JUST
WORDS

HEATHER GODDIN

JUST
WORDS

Heather Goddin

Matador
9 Priory Business Park,
Wistow Road, Kibworth Beauchamp,
Leicestershire. LE8 0RX
Tel: 0116 279 2299
Email: books@troubador.co.uk
Web: www.troubador.co.uk/matador
Twitter: @matadorbooks

ISBN 978 1838592 080
British Library Cataloguing in Publication Data.
A catalogue record for this book is available from the British Library.

Printed and bound by CPI Group (UK) Ltd, Croydon, CR0 4YY
Typeset in 11pt Minion Pro by Troubador Publishing Ltd, Leicester, UK

Matador is an imprint of Troubador Publishing Ltd

For my beloved Christer

JUST WORDS…

I say,
      "I love you."

You say,
      "No, you don't."

And I say,
      "Oh yes, I do."

Just words…
      "I love you."

And I wonder
If you will ever realise
Just how *much* I do.

January 2018

Hummingbirds and Butterflies

I don't even know her name.
Have no idea how old she is.
Older than me, perhaps?
But when I see her in the street,
I think of hummingbirds and butterflies.

Tiny and exquisitely formed,
A handspan waist, a figure like a girl's.
I'm told she was a dancer in her youth,
And when I see her ramrod spine,
The graceful way she walks,
I can believe that, too.

She dresses in the fashions of her youth.
Full-flowing skirts and nipped-in belted waists.
A brilliance of colour and everything to match,
Even her shoes.
Abundance of silk and tulle and lace.
Sometimes a matching flower,
Placed in her high-piled hair.

"Eccentric," say some,
But not to me.
She's keeping up her standards.
She's beautiful and different.
A butterfly amongst the flies.
A hummingbird amongst the crows.

October 2016

NECKLACE

It occurs to me that the memories I have of you
Through the years that I have known you
Are like a necklace made of mismatched stones
But all of equal worth to me.

It grows so long now,
I could wind it several times
Around my neck.

Amongst the stones are garnets, amethysts,
Diamonds, sapphires, emeralds and rubies.
Some are just pebbles and polished stone.
But all, whatever their value,
Are precious to me.

The stones I have added
In the last few days
Are pearls beyond price.

How much longer it can grow,
Now that the days grow short,
Is something I try to forget.

But I shall wear my necklace proudly
All the days of my life.

January 2018

Tearoom in Aldeburgh

I always bring my visitors here.
An old-fashioned tearoom
In the middle of the town.
Real tea in a pot,
With a strainer for the leaves.
The scones the best for miles around.

Today I chose the garden.
Hot sun and partial shade.
A cool breeze from the sea.

Our waiter was a slim, young boy,
With a warm and friendly smile.
Eighteen, nineteen? Twenty, perhaps?

We drank our tea, enjoyed our scones
And slid some coins beneath a plate.
We paid our bill.

As we queued outside the loo,
Our tall, young waiter passed
And smiled at us
That lovely, lovely smile.
Laughing back, I said, in fun,
"If I had been just seventeen,
I would, today, have fallen in love."

Surprised, but pleased, he smiled again,
That devastating smile.
"Thank you for that," he said.
"And thank you for my tip."

There are a *few* good things in being old
For I can *say* at eighty-five
The things I *couldn't* say
At seventeen.

July 2018

WINTER IN CANTABRIA

I think of forests of eucalyptus
Covering the mountains.
Native oaks and chestnuts, not yet quite ousted,
With the last red leaves
Still clinging to their boughs.

I think of pampas grass
Growing along the verges of the motorways
And bright, green, rain-drenched fields
Live with sheep and cows.

I think of a long, deep, limestone gorge.
The darkness of the winding road along the
Pass, with its swollen river driving deep below,
Whilst high above, the mountains glisten in the sun.

I think of old stone houses,
With wooden balconies and carvings underneath the
eaves.
Romanesque churches built of rough-cut stone,
Hiding their golden Baroque treasures from the world
outside.

I think of the Picos deep in snow,
Under a clear, blue sky and sun.
The marshes of the bird reserves
Sheltering migrants from more northern climes.

I think of a wild sea coast,
Its rocky cliffs and golden sands.
The breakers crashing on the shore
And great seas rolling in along the bay.

This, then, is Cantabria,
Its beauty and its dignity.
A warm and courteous people.
Christmas is still Christmas.
Traditional, without the tawdry trappings of today.
Green Spain, I am in love with you.

January 2018

LAS MARISMAS DE SANTONA

Sometimes I see something so beautiful,
It almost takes my breath away.
So it was today, driving across the Causeway,
Between the marshes and the sea.
The sun rose through the mists
In a great, gold aureole of light,
Unearthly and ephemeral,
The distant mountains veiled in cloud,
A solitary heron silhouetted at the water's edge.

These are the moments that I long to share with you.
Wrap them carefully in layers of tissue,
Pack them safely in a well-fitting box
Marked "Fragile",
Mail it off to you and register
To be sure of safe arrival.

How daft is that?
No photograph, no painting and no words
Could ever convey those images
Without we had been there together
To share the moment.

Christmas 2017

For Your Eyes Only

We mourned the demise of flat stomachs,
Slim hips and the firm flesh of youth.
The size of your tummy
Troubles you most.
Why? I don't know,
For you are still *you*.
The trouble is gravity.
Everything drops.
I know that myself.

But I point out to you
That you've still got good legs.
You give me an old-fashioned look.
"And how do you know?"

I smile and reply,
"If you prance round your flat
In your shirt and your pants,
Where else can I look
Apart from your legs?"

How lucky you are.
They are really nice legs.

January 2018

EMPTY ROOMS

When John was in the nursing home,
I visited as often as I could.
I remember a beautiful room
With its views of lawns and trees
That my husband loved so well.

John was luckier than most,
Still had speech and memory
And the company of Ruth
Beside him in her wheelchair,
Unable to move but still young at heart,
With whom he could talk.
But he often fell asleep,
Ruth dozing beside him
And I had time to look around the room.

I saw a sea of sad old faces,
Like empty rooms
From which the occupants had fled.
Yet still I felt some cried for help
From deep inside.
The old man with the restless hands
That drummed upon his chair.
The woman rocking with a doll
As though it were a child.

One day the woman on my other side
Began to weep.
(I never knew her name
Or saw her visitors, if any)
But on that day, her racking sobs
Rang through the silent room
And written on her bland, blank face,
I saw the lines of life and grief and loss.

There was no carer there.
I did the only thing I could.
I took her hand and held it 'til she stopped
And wiped her tears away.
I hoped that in the misty reaches of her mind
She somehow felt that someone cared.
Then, at last, she slept.

Then John and Ruth woke up.
We laughed and talked of many things.
The carers came and tea was served.
Life fell back in place.

She must, my little friend, be long since dead,
Like John and Ruth, as well.
But sometimes, even now, in memory,
I hear her weeping still.

November 2015

PHOTOGRAPHS

In the dark days of winter,
I take out my memories,
Like photographs of summer past.

I see your face, so dear to me,
Smiling or grave, in sunshine and in shade
And I walk once more with you.

So close and yet so far away.
The winter moves with heavy feet.
Next spring when next we meet, eternity away.

November 2012

PROGRESS

Once, this place was beautiful.
I always took my early morning walk
Along the rocky shore
To see the sun rise in its morning loveliness
From the burnished glory of the sea.
From the line of pretty villas round the bay,
The smiling maids called out to me
As they swept the household dust out to the street.
"*Bonju, signurina*. How are you today?"
Even the winter storms were beautiful
When the sun was veiled by cloud
And the bay was lashed by angry waves and spray
And the winter rains flooded the empty streets.

But now the villas are gone,
Replaced by hotels, restaurants and bars.
The rocky shore is strewn with beer cans,
Roaches, used condoms, takeaways.
Fair fruits of last night's discos, bars and clubs.
Congested traffic pumps out poisons to the air
And the heavy rains still flood the streets.
They call it "Progress" now.
Yet whilst the tourists snore in their hotel beds,
The sun still rises and is beautiful.

And, not so far away,
There *are* still places that are beautiful,
Where the tourists and the traffic never go.
Beyond the ever-growing towns and villages
Where the tarmac roads run out,
Amongst the fields and footpaths
That only fishermen and farmers know.
Along the narrow paths beside the edges of the cliffs
Are places with names that read like poetry.
(Mouth of the Wind, The Scythe, The Caves of the
Mares)
Here they *cannot* build,
For the cliffs dive straight as arrows
Down to a frightening sea.
A fall from here and there is no return.

If I could walk (as once I did),
I would come here once again
To see the sun sink into its evening bed
In a blaze of red and gold into a purple sea,
Before the light gives way
To starshine and the dark.

But if, en route,
I met a farmer working in his fields,
Would he smile and say,
"*Bonju, Sinjura,*"
As once he would have done?
Probably not.
For after all,
There is now this thing called "Progress".

June 2018

DISAPPOINTMENT

Why does it always happen to me?

If I sit in the sun, I burn.
If I walk in the rain, I drown.
I lose my way in mist and fog.
I break both legs on the ice.

Some people rant and rave,
Flaunting their wounds for others to see.
I sit quietly with my set-sphinx smile,
Hiding the hurt inside.

Life's kicked me in the teeth again.
So what do I do now?
Continue to follow my dream,
Pick myself up and start again,
Just as I always do.

March 2012

Bloody Men (For Shirley Field)

A friend said to me,
"All men are bastards,
Even the best."
And I would agree.
Amen to that.

What do we see in them?
Telling us lies just for the fun of it?
Tearing off wings from the innocent butterflies?
Trampling on feelings in their hard hob-nailed boots?
Thoughtless and blind,
Cowards and hypocrites,
Little tin gods.

What do they want from us?
(Apart from the obvious.)
A mother? A punch bag?
Someone to booster their egos?

Are they afraid of us?
Oh yes, they are.
Would put us in cages
To keep us restrained.
Knickers to that!

So why? What the hell then,
Do we poor silly cows
Need to put up with it?

We just fall in love.
Can't live without them.

November 2015

BLACKBIRD AND WHITE CAT

The white cat sits at the gate,
Never coming any closer,
Defying me from a distance.

I sit in the warm evening sun,
Glass of wine in hand,
Watching the midsummer daisies sway in the breeze,
Waiting for my evening recital to begin.

Then suddenly, he's there,
My opera star,
High on the gable of a neighbour's house,
Starting his performance with bravura trills,
Showing off for all the world to hear.
I wait, entranced. The cat has other motives.

No ordinary bird. A consummate musician.
Mime as well as singer.
The calls of crow and gull. A mewing cat.
Threaded between the passages of glorious song,
The coloratura scales and fluting notes,
To which he's added, joy of joys,
The ringtone of a mobile phone.
I watch that open yellow beak and quivering throat,
Until he takes his bow and flies away.

The longest day is past and summer heightens.
The midsummer daisies fade and soon will die.
The blackbird's songs will disappear.
Will he come back to take up residence next year?
Will he have learnt to sing me something new?
Shall I be here to listen?

I empty my glass and go to cook my meal.
The white cat lingers on.
Staring at the birds and licking his lips.

July 2018

WOLVES

Our guide had said,
"If you go walking in these woods,
You might come face to face with wolves."
And he explained they had been reintroduced
To a different part of Switzerland
And they had spread to other regions of the Alps.

The hotel stood high, below the woods and towering
crags.
Far, far below lay Lake Lucerne.
The sun shone out of a clear, blue sky,
On range upon range of mountain peaks.

That night was hot.
I found it hard to sleep
And rose at dawn to sit outside,
Out on my balcony,
To watch the sun rise through the mists,
Gilding the mountain snows.

Then a dog began to howl
In the village down below, or so I thought.
Another dog joined in
And then a third, a fourth and several more.
Then something said to me,
"These are not dogs. They're wolves
Calling from the woods above."

That evening, talking to a fellow guest,
She said, "I know that this sounds daft,
But I thought that I heard wolves last night,
Howling in the woods."
I told her that I'd heard it too.
We laughed and said, in unison,
"I wonder if we did?"

I wonder still.
I hope we did.

August 2018

THE WAITING GAME

I, who leap headlong, impulsive,
Am having to play the waiting game.

In this North Sea town beside a quiet sea,
I watch the seagulls fighting over food.
I envy them their simple lives.
They hatch, they breed, they die.
They do not have to play, like me,
The endless waiting game.

Loving you will never be easy,
I knew that from the start,
And distance is a barrier
That is very hard to climb.
The days grow shorter every year.
I do not have the time to play
This deadly waiting game.

So, I shall continue to send you my letters
And wait for your replies.
Stifling my impatience
With the hated waiting game.

Your letter arrived this morning.

September 2007

COOKING A POEM

People sometimes ask me,
"How long does it take
To write a poem?"

And I say that it varies.
Poems are like cooking,
Sometimes like using the microwave,
Ideas assembled and ready to cook.
"Ping" and its done
In no time at all.

But, often, there's need of a crockpot.
Like making a casserole.
Ideas at the back of my mind,
Needing to marinate meat,
Drowned in cognac and wine
For quite a long time.
When it's finally ready,
Then into the pot goes the poem
With the other ingredients
For a long, slow cooking time.

Later, rather than sooner,
I add some words, like herbs,
Or a drop more wine
And more seasoning.
Then on I go,
Until I'm satisfied.
When you're cooking a stew in a crockpot,
Time adds to the flavour.

And that's how it is with some poems.
A tweak here and there.
Some substitute words?
I just go on cooking,
Until it feels right.

January 2018

HILLS

When I come amongst them,
The hills excite me.
On clear blue days when they cut into the sky,
I want to reach out and hold them.
Feel their shapes beneath my hands.
Compare those shapes to bones below the skin.

On hazy, wet or foggy days,
When their shapes are undefined,
I feel their deeper flesh,
Veiling the bones.
And I fancy that if I leant against them,
I would feel softness with the strength
Against my back.

And when I see them stretching away
Into the dim blue distance,
I think of them as some great feather bed,
Where I might sleep
And dream away my fears.

As a child, when I drew the four-square house,
With smoke rising from its chimneys,
Which then most children did,
Always in the background I drew hills,
Where linear birds flew overhead.

Now grounded on flat land,
Surmounted by vast skies,
I long for the hills.
The hills excite me.
When I come amongst them,
I am come home.

October 2018

HOME

This is a place with cupboards to hang up my clothes
And a bed where I lay down my head.
Shelves for my china and glass
And a place for my pots and my pans.
Fridges and freezers to store all my food.
A washing machine, a table and chairs.
Somewhere to eat and to sleep.
Survival, not living.

This is a place with a roof
To keep out the rain.
Windows to let in the light.
Something to clean and keep tidy,
Banishing spiders and laying the dust.
A place to keep warm.
And for what?

It is a place of cluttered emptiness,
A prison from which I want to escape.
Yet sometimes a refuge from life
When the world becomes too much.

Home is a person.
Not a place.

August 2008

LYRIDS

I was born on a night of the Lyrids.
Perhaps that is why I love the meteors,
Bright arrows of the dark.
So much better than fireworks,
Because they are silent
And owe nothing to art or man.
So here I sit in the garden,
With only owl and fox for company,
Fixing my gaze upon the skies,
Thinking of infinity.

Thick and fast they come, the meteors.
First one way, then another.
Tumbling and dancing
Across the midnight sky.
Sudden and amazing,
Making me catch my breath
With the unexpected joy of it.

"Wish upon a falling star", they say.
I have counted forty-one tonight.
Wished the same wish every time.
Then waited for the next.
And I shall tell no one what I wished.
In case it never comes true.
In any case, they'd probably have guessed wrong.

September 2007

THE KISS

I dreamt you came and kissed me in the night,
The pressure of your lips on mine
Tender, erotic, strong.
Awakening from the depths of me
What had been dormant for so long.
Like water sourced from water deep below the earth,
Struggling to reach the light, the sun, the sky.

And in the darkness when I woke,
Although you are so far away,
I felt you, briefly, close to me,
Before I fell asleep.

April 2009

THE DANCE

I sometimes think that our letters
Are like the measures of some ancient stately dance.
Advance and retreat.
A step to the side.
Retreat and advance.
Circle and turn.
Weaving the careful patterns of the dance.
No hint of love,
Save the message in the eyes,
The touch of hands,
The language of the fan.

My letters to you are letters of love,
Where yet no word of love is said
And yours to me so full of warmth.
They set my spirits flying.
But, like me, you keep to the rules of the dance.

Soon the music will stop.
There will be an interval.
We shall be together
Outside the limits of the dance.
What, if anything, happens then, I wonder?

August 2008

In Praise of Snores

I lie awake and listen to the snores.
Now, past the homicidal stage,
I try instead to analyse
Each episode of snores.

At first, the pleasant lowing of the cows
In some far-distant field.
Quite gentle, this.
It is relaxed and sometimes I can sleep.

But now a fiercer note is heard.
The roar of lions and tigers in the wild.
The trumpeting of elephants,
Not far enough away.

Then, next we have the racing cars,
Revving and roaring round the track.
Sometimes the engines will cut out
And then, such blessed peace.

But worst of all, the jolly pigs,
Ecstatic round the trough.
Whistling and gurgling in the other bed,
Grunting and snorting right beside my ear,
All culminating in a fearsome scream.
(Blood-curdling dreams of abattoirs, perhaps?)
Enough to wake the dead.

Tonight there was a new event.
A long, slow hiss and rattle.
A cobra or a rattlesnake
Uncoiling in the nearby bed?
I don't think I can cope with that.
I'm terrified of snakes.

Ah, this is not just snoring.
It's wall-to-wall, pure deep-pile sound.
Oh, Champion of Champions,
To you must go the prize.

March 2009

ARBOREAL IMAGING

Apart from the glorious Ardennes,
The countryside of Belgium is so dull.
Flat fields and unattractive villages.
Maybe you have to know it well
To love it.
I gaze from a window of the coach
And struggle not to fall asleep.

Then all at once, in the middle of a field,
I see a line of trees. Six in a perfect row.
So uniform. Just like a chorus line.
I half expect to see them raise their limbs in unison,
In a froth of emerald leaves.

Wild flights of fancy pull me wide awake.
I start to look at trees quite differently.
This is a lovely game to play to pass the time.
Better than eating crisps or chocolate.

I see two trees together in each other's shade,
Their branches close entwined.
Two young lovers, perhaps,
Lost in their perfect dream?

A triangle. One tree further off.
Is it an eternal one,
Or just "Two's company, three's a crowd"?

A big tree and a little one,
So much alike that they can only be
Proud mother and her sturdy child.

And then a wood with one tree set apart.
A singer with an audience?
A vicar preaching to his flock?

A small copse of assorted trees,
A tall pine in its midst.
A teacher with his pupils on a trip?
A tour guide with his group?

Amazing how the time then flew.
We seemed to reach the ferry
In just no time at all.

July 2018

CHIARETTO FOR BREAKFAST

This is the ultimate luxury place.
Everything geared to pamper and indulge.
Beautiful food and excellent service.
Huge bedroom. Vast comfortable bed.
(Nine types of pillow from which you can choose
If the first one doesn't suit?)
A balcony looking on immaculate grounds
And a view of the lake.
Everything planned to modern good taste.
Technology all up to date.

Not quite, perhaps, what I'd have chosen.
I'd have preferred something less perfect,
With old-fashioned charm.
But I have to admit that for just a few days,
It's good to be pampered in filmstar-like style.

But the best thing of all
Is the huge buffet breakfast.
A wondrous selection of fruit,
Platters of meats and of cheeses.
(Even the full "greasy" English.)
Croissants and cakes
And all kinds of bread.

And deep in a corner stand, several bottles

Of a fizzy pink drink.
"A glass of Chiaretto for breakfast," they say,
"Is good for the health."
So whilst I stay here,
I'll continue to take
A glassful each morning
With my croissant or cake
And *know* I'll keep well
Through the cold winter days.

Lago di Garda, Christmas 2018

Lago di Garda

I sit in the sun beside the lake on Christmas Eve,
Watching the pristine-feathered gulls
And coal-black cormorants.

Three yachts in a stately measured line
Sail by, on a background of misty light
And I think of that old English carol,
"I saw three ships come sailing by
On Christmas Day, on Christmas Day."

And then a cormorant perched on a buoy
Opens his wings in a strange evocation
Of things to come.
The Crucifixion,
Reminders of birth and death,
All within moments.

It has been a beautiful day.
Bardolino, Garda, Lazise.
I had forgotten how lovely Italy is
And the warmth of its people.

I recall encounters in the Christmas markets.
The silversmith who had worked in London,
Selling his wares to the John Lewis partnership.
The handsome young man from Brescia,
From whom I bought my "vin brulee",
Who told me of his dream to make enough money
To buy a house in his much-loved town
Just to be near his mother.

A lovely day.
Yet sitting here,
I feel such longing for your presence
That I want to cry,
As I cannot share these things with you
On Christmas Eve.

Christmas 2018

ROSE

No man has ever sent me flowers.
Not even you.
But once you sent a birthday card.
A rose, a perfect rose,
So fresh and beautiful,
That from the printed page
I almost breathed its scent.

Was it a conscious choice
Or just coincidence?
I never know for sure
The thoughts that cross your mind.

But when I rang to thank you for the card,
I praised the rose and said to you
That that was better than the real.
And you took up my words and said to me,
"Yes. Real flowers fade.
The card will always last."

So, now I feel
The way I did
When first I drew it from the envelope.
That this is the message of the rose
And I shall keep that card
Until the day I die.

April 2010

CHACONNE (ATTRIB. TOMASO VITALI)

It stops me in its tracks
Whenever I hear it played.
Draws me into it
And moves me deeply.
Makes its sorrows my own.
Almost too much to bear.

In the hands of a maestro,
The solo violin weeps and laments,
Weaving its patterns of sorrow
Against the slow, relentless, tragic theme,
Taking me to a no man's land of emptiness,
Aching grief and loss.

Yet, as the piece unfolds and moves towards its close,
Gaining in strength and resolution all the while,
As violin and orchestra unite,
I feel the triumph of the human soul
Fighting back against adversity,
With a great defiant affirmation
Of hope in the face of despair.

August 2011

The Fount of Youth

You tell me you are old.
I know you are
And so am I.
But when I look at you,
I don't see age.
I just see *you*.
Ageless and invincible.

No matter that our bodies age,
We lose our strength or live with pain,
We cannot do what once we did,
The fount of youth in both of us
Still rises from within.

I see in you
The eager boy that once you were.
I hope you see in me
The laughing girl that once was I.
With childlike joy we greet each day.
We still have faith and hope and love.

April 2010

COURTING COUPLE

From my window, I watch them every day.
A pair. Not yet a couple.
He, so proud and elegant,
In dazzling white and clerical grey,
Against the drabness of the sky,
Strutting his stuff along the parapet.

She is smaller. No less beautiful.
Her steps are shorter and more delicate,
Provocative and feminine.
She flirts tail feathers black and purest white,
Ruffled in the south-west wind.

They sit along the terrace wall.
Side by side, just feet apart,
Or back to back like bookends on a shelf,
Making small sounds through yellow beaks.
But she is playing hard to get.
If he comes too close, she hustles him away.
Then he takes flight and circles high above,
Calls to her raucously loud and clear.
Sometimes she comes. Sometimes she does not.
She is not ready to commit.

I watch them every day, my herring gulls
And soon I must be gone.
But I feel so sure that very soon,
As spring progresses in the bay,
That there will be a clutch of eggs
On a ledge along the cliffs.

March 2011

THE LITTLE MERMAID

When I come to think of it,
I have lived with pain of one kind or another
All the days of my life.
But physical pain can concentrate the mind.
Diminishes all other kinds of pain.

Yet there are compensations.
When in the company of those I love,
I rise above the pain, forgetting self.
I feel that if I rose and ran,
The pain of years would fall away.
Reality, I fear, is something else.

And when I plod my painful way along a street,
Gritting my teeth and counting my steps,
I think of the Little Mermaid, who, for love,
Took on the burden of having legs,
When every step felt like treading on knives
And all for a prince who never noticed her.

If I had been her,
I would have asked for something else.
I would have asked for wings.
How *then*, could he *not* have noticed her?
But I guess that wings must also have their snags.
Moult, perhaps, leaving her grounded.
Or mechanical failure in mid-air?
There is a price to pay
For everything.

July 2011

CINDERELLA

When I was little,
I wanted to wear a pretty long dress
And go to a ball.

Then, in my teens,
It was my school friends who went to the dinners and
balls.
I sat at home on Saturday nights,
With my parents, a book and the cat.
We listened to radio, went to bed early,
Long before midnight, of course.
There was no money to buy a long dress,
But nobody asked me to go to a ball.

Now I am old,
I have lovely long dresses,
But dinners and balls are thin on the ground
And don't come my way.

Perhaps that's as well,
For I just couldn't walk,
Let alone dance,
In the little glass slippers.

November 2018

REAR WINDOW

I live in a lonely place of darkened fields at night,
With only distant points of light
And I never see a soul.

I've never stayed in a flat before
And I find I rather like it.
Like being in *Rear Window*
Without James Stewart and Grace Kelly
And the thrilling vistas into other peoples' lives.
(I'm no voyeur!)
No wheelchairs, dramas, murders on the block.
Some potted plants on window sills,
A Christmas tree or two
And lighted windows round the square.
I love to think of lives lived out behind the panes
And know I'm not alone.

Yours are the first lights on
Across the courtyard opposite.
I am an early riser, too.
I am awake, long, long before my hosts have stirred.
You make your breakfast then
About the time I go to make my tea.
That's when I raise my blind, switch on my light
And wave across to you.
(Sometimes you wave first.
Once you've seen my light come on.)
It is our morning ritual.

I lie awake a while,
Thinking of the things
That we planned to do today.
These are my precious moments.
I shall miss them when I leave.

Now, I am back with the darkened fields
And the distant points of light.
And I miss you, I miss you,
I miss you.

January 2019

NEVER

I often dream when I take the bus
Around the countryside I know and love,
That there is still a chance
That someday you will come
And I try to see the places through your eyes.
The bus is fun and you would love it too.
You would enjoy the drivers and the "regulars"
Whom I have come to know as friends.

Once you might have come
When you were still active,
But you were reluctant to commit
And always far too busy.
Now I fear it is too late
And you will never come.

Would you come if I was dying?
Probably not.
It is too far to come
And getting around is now so difficult.
For you it is too late
And you would never come.

Would you come to my funeral?
Possibly, yes,
If you were still able to travel.
But the dead don't need the living.
The living do.

So, I'll continue to dream,
As I travel the bus
Through the pretty villages,
The fields, the woods,
The marshes and the sea.
And I try to kid myself
That one day you will come.

Never is the saddest word I know.

January 2019

GREY DAY ON GOZO

I sit here idly listening to the wind,
Watching the dark clouds race across the sky.
Catching odd gleams of silver from a fleeting sun
Between the showers of heavy rain.
The ferry boats are wallowing deep
In white-topped waves on stormy seas.

I sit here, simply missing you.
Knowing an aching need of you,
Remembering happy days,
Wanting your laughter and your smile.

All I can do is will the time to pass quickly
Until we meet again.

February 2010

AT CHRISTMAS

Spare a thought at Christmas
For those who are alone.
Those who are old or sick.
Those without family and whose friends are dead,
Estranged from children, waiting in the wings,
For an unloved parent to die.

I think of someone changing their clothes,
Filling their kettle, mince pies close at hand,
Waiting in hope that someone will come
Or the telephone will ring.
But no one comes and no one rings.

Spare a thought at Christmas
For those who have no home,
Through no fault of their own.
Destitute and desperate,
Sleeping rough on pavements,
Huddled in a blanket, no pillow for their head,
Facing the elements, too far gone to care,
Whilst people scurry by, abusing them,
Or pretending not to see.

Spare a thought at Christmas
For those less fortunate than us.
Reach out a hand to help, if you can.
There but for the grace of God
Go all of us.

Christmas Day 2013

MARMALADE (FOR IRENE AND CHRIS)

Now you are no more.
Your nine lives are used up.
But oh, how well you used those lives.
Twenty-two years.
My neighbours' cat.

A fearless hunter in his prime.
Kept us free from rats and mice,
The rabbit population down.
Only last year, he caught an old cock pheasant
Bigger than himself.
I try to forget the robins and the fledgling birds.

He was very beautiful.
Big and bold and arrogant.
Bright, silken, ginger fur,
Trimmed with purest white.
Emperor and master of his neighbourhood
And justly so.

But he was also lovable,
Everybody's friend.
He liked to sit beside me in the sun
Or on the wall whilst I waited for the bus.
Sociable and curious.
He supervised my groceries on my return,
In case there might be something there
That was just meant for him.
He met me often from the bus.
Caused comment from the passengers.
They knew him well.

My gardener will grieve for him.
(He has six cats himself.)
Brought him biscuits every week.
I'll swear his Lordship knew the time
That he was due,
For he was always there.

I watched him grow so old and thin.
The silken coat grow coarse and sparse.
He slept away his days.
But still, each morning, there was he,
The small face peering in,
Scrabbling his dirty paws upon the glass,
Demanding entry and a saucer of milk.
Telling me, the fibber, he was starved
Of food by those he loved.
Wilful and wicked to the last.

Oh, how we will miss you, Marmalade.
May you sleep well, my feline friend,
In the garden that you loved.

April 2014

Something You Said

Out of the blue you said, accusingly,
"You won't let anything stop you
From doing what you want to do."
Surprised, I laughed and agreed.
And then I said, "Neither do *you*.
It's true of both of us."

I should have said but didn't,
"Yes, I agree, but I draw the line
At causing hurt.
I lack that streak of ruthlessness,
Which is why I never win
And never gain
The things I want the most."

How is it with you?

February 2014

HJORTHAGEN CHURCH

I love this place.
I love its simple grace and calm.
Grey-painted pews, the frieze above the chancel arch.
The golden deer beside the chancel steps.
Whilst from the stained-glass windows high above
Christ in Glory smiles down on us below.

I love this place.
I love the hymns, so many that I have not heard.
The organ there, supporting us
And even in a language that I do not know,
The prayers to which I listen but I cannot say,
God's grace is there to fill me with His peace.

I love this place.
The fellowship of friends who smile at me
And make me welcome in their midst,
So I feel God's grace is there with us.
So many churches seem to close themselves to me.
Hjorthagen takes me to its heart.

July 2012

THE DEATH OF CLEOPATRA

The music drew me from another room.
A voice so beautiful it blotted out all other thought.
A recording made in Amsterdam
Some years ago.
Berlioz. "The Death of Cleopatra."
I had heard it once or twice before,
But never like this.

I had heard her sing a long time back
And when I heard that recently,
She had sung *Norma* and *Salome*
In opera houses round the world.
I wondered how the mezzo voice
Would deal with those two roles.
Now I know that both of them
Would have been sublime.

I stood transfixed and listened
To that flawless voice.
The notes that sent shivers down my spine.
She gave me Cleopatra's passion and her grief
And made them mine.
A consummate artist.
A truly great musician.

Into the silence that followed the music's close
Fell the voice of my hostess,
Speaking with pride and wonderment,
Something almost like awe,
"And this is my daughter!"

January 2019

OLD MAN IN A WHITE SUMMER HAT

He stood at my stall, eyes upon my books.
An old man in a white summer hat.
Ninety, at least, but still upright and tall.
"Do you like poetry?" I said.
He cupped a hand to his ear and said,
"You must excuse me. I am very deaf."
I repeated my question and he said,
"Yes, I do. Very much."
He picked up a book. Put on his spectacles.
He smiled. "Blind as well," he said
And then began to read.

Out of the crowd came a woman,
Younger than he.
I saw the radiance in their faces as they met
And their exchange of smiles.
He thrust the book into her hands
And said, "Read that. The first one in the book."
It was a poem about love.
And in that moment, I knew that that was how he felt
About her.

He handed me a note.
I gave him change and signed the title page.
He shook my hand. Gave me a smile.
Then slowly, arm in arm, they walked away.
I shall never forget them.

It is moments like these
That make writing poetry
All worthwhile.

July 2018

GIANT'S COUNTERPANE

Usually, when I arrive in winter,
The clouds hide the land
And I only catch glimpses
Of this much-loved place.
Of little red houses, woods and fields.
The occasional frozen lake.

But today the sun is shining
Out of a clear blue sky.
The ground below looks like a giant's counterpane.
The land around as far as the eye can see
White with snow.
A quilt with an abstract pattern,
Embroidered with blue for shadows
Of the sun on snow.
Brown for bare trees and grey for the lakes
And where the sun falls on glass or ice,
There are gleams of gold and silver thread.
I am totally entranced.

Only a thousand feet or so above the ground
Do the clouds drive in.
But I've had my minutes of beauty
And now we are landed.

January 2019

SUNDAY BREAKFAST

Long ago, when first we met,
We breakfasted together in a hotel dining room
With a panoramic view.
Views across the island.
A room where we could watch the skies
And gauge the weather for the day ahead
Or see the cruise ships dock below.

An uninspiring breakfast.
Ham and cheese, salami, bread.
Sometimes tinned fruit salad.
But I livened it up with honey, brought from home,
And breakfasting with you
Was the perfect start to every day.

Now, today, on Sunday,
I'm eating breakfast in your flat,
So that we'll have lots of time
To get to church without a rush.

And what a lovely breakfast!
The kitchen table laid so beautifully.
The breakfast candles lit.
So many types of *knäckerbröd*
And different kinds of lovely bread.
A big wedge of your favourite cheese.
(All you had added to your daily choice
Were wafer-thin turkey and thin-cut ham.)
And honey in a jar, reminding me of Malta long ago.
Plenty of tea from a large homely pot.

Breakfasting with you, just as in Malta,
Is still the perfect way
To start my day.

January 2019

The Wee House in the Churchyard

A winding tarmac path leads to its door.
Discreetly set behind the church.
Close to the peaceful dead and a line of lime trees'
shade,
Indigenous, tar-timbered walls and red roof tiles,
This wee house now is ours.

Within its doors, palatial space.
Disabled access, baby-changing unit.
Pristine fittings, pipework, basin.
Best of all, the noble throne,
Fit for a bishop or a queen.
And who will have the honour of first flush?
The Vicar? A celebrity?
Or just some desperate soul in need?
The answer is… the architect.

June 2013

A piece of lavatory humour written for the inauguration ceremony of the long-
awaited church facilities at All Saints Church, Darsham on 16 June 2013.

Under the Umbrella

I love to walk with you in rain.
You take my arm
And draw me into you
Under the umbrella.

I feel the warmth and inner strength of you.
My poor, enchanted heart
Flutters against your arm,
Like some wild and captive bird.

I love to be with you at any time,
But when it rains, I never want the rain to stop,
For I never feel more cherished or protected
Than under the umbrella.

October 2009

BETWEEN THE FOURTH FLOOR AND THE GROUND

Last night, between the fourth floor and the ground,
You bent your head and kissed me on the mouth.
Not passionate, not lingering, but firm
And long enough for my response.
I softly pressed my lips to yours,
Until we gently broke apart.

And this was you.
Slow-burner that you are.
The man who told me, long ago,
"I never kiss upon the lips these days.
I have forgotten how."
Who always turned his face away,
In case my goodnight kiss upon his cheek
Strayed out of bounds.

But you kissed me in that rickety lift
Or did I dream it all,
Sleeping on my feet, like a horse,
For the brief time that it takes
From the fourth floor to the ground?
But I *know* that it happened
And you kissed me on the mouth.
Rusty, perhaps, from lack of use,
But you haven't forgotten how.

Nothing was said
When you walked me to my bus,
Apart from arrangements for the following day
And my goodnight kiss upon your cheek
Was firmly back in place.

Soon we must part again
And I will miss you, as I always do,
But I shall have a memory
Of a moment of joy in a vintage lift,
Between the fourth floor and the ground.

April 2018

AT THE NEW YEAR

I stand at the edge of the year,
Watching the past fall away.
Something is happening,
Not yet explained or fully understood,
From which there can be now no turning back.
Unsure of the future, yet ready to go,
For good or ill,
My life will never be the same again.

The winds of change are blowing through my life,
Opening doors I never knew were there.
I can see brightness in the sky
Beyond the windows of my mind.
The darkest clouds have rolled away
And promise me a glorious day.

31st December 2007

ACKNOWLEDGEMENTS

My grateful thanks to Robert and Denise Vanston who printed the poems out for me and to Irene Beager who proof read them.